Basketball Rules
IN PICTURES

Edited by **A. G. Jacobs**

Consultant: **Paul "Frosty" Francis, Jr.**
EXECUTIVE DIRECTOR, INTERNATIONAL ASSOCIATION
OF APPROVED BASKETBALL OFFICIALS, INC.

Illustrated by George Kraynak

A GD/PERIGEE BOOK

Perigee Books
are published by
The Putnam Publishing Group
200 Madison Avenue
New York, New York 10016

Library of Congress catalog card number: 63-12937
ISBN 0-399-50973-9

First Perigee printing, 1983
Printed in the United States of America
    2 3 4 5 6 7 8 9

*Dedicated to
the hard-working officials—too
often more blamed than praised*

The English language does not have a singular pronoun which denotes both
male and female; therefore *he, him,* and *his* are used throughout this book
and refer to both men and women.

The rules depicted herein are those of the National Collegiate Athletic Association. The rules of the National Federation of State High School Associations may differ in a few instances.

INTRODUCTION

The game of basketball was invented in 1891 by Dr. James A. Naismith, an instructor at the International Young Men's Christian Association Training School (now Springfield College) in Springfield, Massachusetts. He did so at the suggestion of Dr. Luther H. Gulick, head of the YMCA physical training staff, who had become concerned over the drop in the club's attendance during the winter months. The cause, he reasoned, was that there was no competitive winter athletic program, the chief means by which the YMCA recruited its members. The problem of creating an indoor team game to compete with the outdoor varieties was turned over to Dr. Naismith.

Dr. Naismith studied the existing outdoor team games and came to several conclusions. First, most team games used a ball which was either hit or driven toward a goal; but if a ball were used indoors, it would have to be light and large, for safety and control. Second, most outdoor team sports emphasized roughness and physical contact, which would be highly dangerous indoors, so running with the ball and physical contact were eliminated. Third, the roughest play in outdoor sports occurred when both teams congregated near a goal; this possible danger was eliminated by placing the goal above the heads of the contestants. Dr. Naismith used two empty peach baskets as goals, threw in a soccer ball, and basketball was born.

The inventor established 13 basic rules, which were written out and posted on the bulletin board for all to see. These rules remained the basic rules of the game for the next fifty years.

The simplicity, logic, and adaptability of basketball gave impetus to its acceptance and popularity, and by 1913 the rules were printed in 30 languages and there were an estimated 20,000,000 players throughout the world.

Today basketball is one of the most popular sports in the world, and it is safe to say that almost every man, woman, and child in the United States under 75 years of age has played it at one time or another and is at least vaguely familiar with its rules. Television has increased its popularity as a spectator sport, and its designation as an Olympic event has given it status as one of the world's great sports. The International Association of Approved Basketball Officials is an organization which is filling a worldwide need of clarifying and interpreting the application of the rules of the game.

This book, in its small way, is intended to help the beginner understand the game of basketball as it is played today. It is by no means complete, and each player, spectator, or television viewer is advised to read the rules printed in the back of the book, as a supplement to the complete rule book.

Throughout the book we have used the letter R to denote Referee, and U to denote Umpire; the Lead Official is indicated by the letter L and the Trail Official by the letter T. In the drawings, the team with the white jerseys is the offensive team.

The editor wishes to express sincere appreciation to Mr. John P. Nucatola, Mr. Bruce Basset, and Mr. Paul "Frosty" Francis, Jr., Executive Director of IAABO, for their ever-available help in making this book possible.

A. G. Jacobs

For those who are, or will soon be, using the metric system, we enclose the following chart.

U.S. to Metric

> All answers are to two decimal places. Therefore if you are going to convert a number not directly shown, it can be found by the addition of two or three numbers. When adding to reach your total, be sure that the decimal point is always moved two places to the left.

INCHES to CM		FEET to METERS		CU. YDS. to CU. METERS		MILES to KM	
U.S.	Metric	U.S.	Metric	U.S.	Metric	U.S.	Metric
1	2.54	1	.30	1	.76	1	1.61
2	5.08	2	.61	2	1.53	2	3.22
3	7.62	3	.91	3	2.29	3	4.83
4	10.16	4	1.22	4	3.06	4	6.44
5	12.70	5	1.52	5	3.82	5	8.05

CONTENTS

BASKETBALL

THE GAME

Basketball is played by two teams of five players each. The purpose of each team is to throw the ball into its own basket and to prevent the other team from scoring. The ball may be thrown, batted, rolled or dribbled in any direction, subject to restrictions laid down in the following rules.

THE BASKETBALL COURT

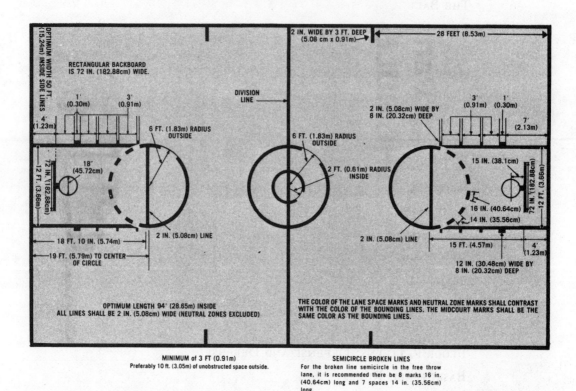

COURT DIMENSIONS

HIGH SCHOOL: 50 feet wide by 84 feet long.
COLLEGE: 50 feet wide by 94 feet long.
    The playing court should be clearly marked with sidelines and end lines. There shall be *at least* 3 feet of unobstructed space outside the lines (ten feet is preferable).

THE BALL

SPECIFICATIONS, COLOR

The ball shall be spherical. Its color shall be the approved orange shade. For college games, it shall have a leather cover unless the teams agree to use a ball with a composition cover. It shall be of the molded type. If the panels are leather, they shall be cemented to the spherically molded fabric which surrounds an airtight rubber lining. Channels and/or seams shall not exceed one-fourth inch [0.64cm] in width. Its circumference shall be within a maximum of 30 inches [76.2cm] and a minimum of 29½ inches [74.93cm]. Its weight shall not be less than 20 ounces [567.0g] nor more than 22 ounces [623.7g]. It shall be inflated to an air pressure such that when it is dropped to the playing surface from a height of six feet [1.83m], measured to the bottom of the ball, it will rebound to a height, measured to the top of the ball, of not less than 49 inches [124.46cm] when it strikes on its least resilient spot nor more than 54 inches [137.16cm] when it strikes on its most resilient spot.

NOTE—*To be legal, a ball must be tested for resilience at the factory and the air pressure which will give the required reaction must be stamped on it. The pressure for game use must be such as to make the ball bounce legally.*

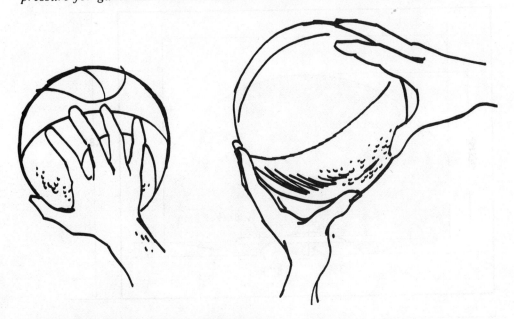

CIRCUMFERENCE OF THE BALL

BELOW SENIOR HIGH SCHOOLS: a minimum of 29 inches and a maximum of 29½ inches.
ADULTS: a minimum of 29½ inches and a maximum of 30 inches.
The home team provides the ball, which must meet the specifications of the rules.

THE BASKETS

The metal single ring is 18 inches in inside diameter. Each basket has 12 attachment loops. The basket is so constructed that the ball is checked momentarily as it passes through the white cord or plastic mesh net. The ring is securely attached to the backboard. The upper edge of the rim is 10 feet above and parallel to the floor, and is equidistant from the vertical edges of the backboard. Ring and attaching flange are orange.

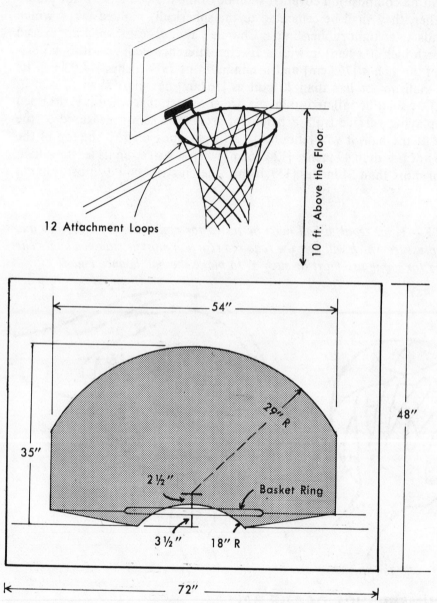

THE BACKBOARDS

The material used for the backboards should be rigid, flat, and either white or transparent. The dimensions are:
RECTANGULAR BACKBOARD: 4 feet vertically by 6 feet horizontally.
FAN-SHAPED BACKBOARD: 54 inches wide at the widest point.

BEFORE THE GAME

Approximately ten minutes before game time, the officials bring the opposing captains to the center of the floor for introductions. The Referee is responsible for bringing the visiting captain and the Umpire brings the captain of the home team. After introductions the Referee briefly explains any ground rules and indicates the color each team will be called (the color of the team's jersey).

To start the game the Referee tosses the ball in the air at the center of the court. It is the Referee's duty to see that the toss is straight and that the ball is not tapped until it reaches its full height. After the toss the Referee stands in place and allows all of the ten players to go ahead of him. He then assumes the position of the Trail Official. The Umpire leads the play after the jump ball and is called the Lead Official. The coverage is similar at all three jump circles.

LENGTH OF GAME

Professional	four 12-minute quarters	15 minutes rest between halves 90 seconds between other quarters and for time outs.
College	two halves of 20 minutes each	15 minutes between halves
High School	four 8-minute quarters	10 minutes between halves 1 minute following 1st and 3rd quarters
Young players	four 6-minute quarters	10 minutes between halves 1 minute following 1st and 3rd quarters

HANDLING AND ADVANCING THE BALL

There are many ways of moving the ball down the floor. The best method of insuring accuracy is to control the ball with the tips of the fingers. This holds true for throwing, batting, receiving, shooting, dribbling, etc.

A player may choose to use one of many passes — depending on his ability and the play situation. He may choose to use a one- or two-handed bounce pass, a backward bounce pass, a one- or two-handed push pass, a chest pass, or a pass of his own creation.

THE ONE-HANDED PASS

This pass is not too accurate but is useful in getting the ball down the length of the court.

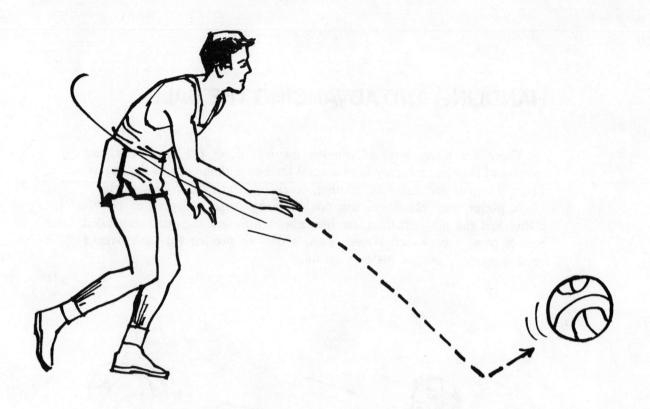

THE BOUNCE PASS

The bounce pass is used most often in pivot plays.

THE TWO-HANDED CHEST PASS

This is the most accurate of the various passes. The step forward on the two-handed chest pass helps produce a good follow through.

HANDING THE BALL

A player may hand the ball to a teammate.

THE DRIBBLE

The dribble is ball movement by a player who throws or taps the ball in the air or onto the floor and then touches it once or several times or catches it.

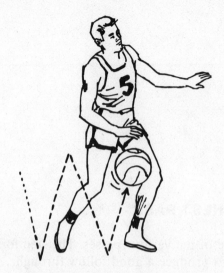

A player sometimes uses a high bounce in the dribble for speed when he is primarily interested in getting the ball down the court.

The same player might use a low bounce in the dribble for more accuracy or when in a relatively tight situation, such as when trying to get around his opponent or when trying to knife in toward the basket for a lay-up shot.

The dribble ends when: (1) the dribbler catches the ball with one or both hands; (2) the dribbler touches the ball with both hands simultaneously; (3) the opponent bats the ball; and (4) the dribbler is unable to immediately catch or continue to dribble the ball.

FLOOR POSITION

A player is entitled to a normal floor position not occupied by an opponent, provided he does not cause personal contact by taking such a position.

THE SCREEN PASS

A player may use a screen, which is a legal action of having another player, without causing contact, delay or prevent an opponent from reaching a desired position.

SHOOTING

Shots for the basket may be made from anywhere on the court. A player may choose from a variety of shots the one best suited to the game situation or to his special abilities.

A two-hand set shot.

A one-hand set shot.

A tap-in shot (not a true shot).

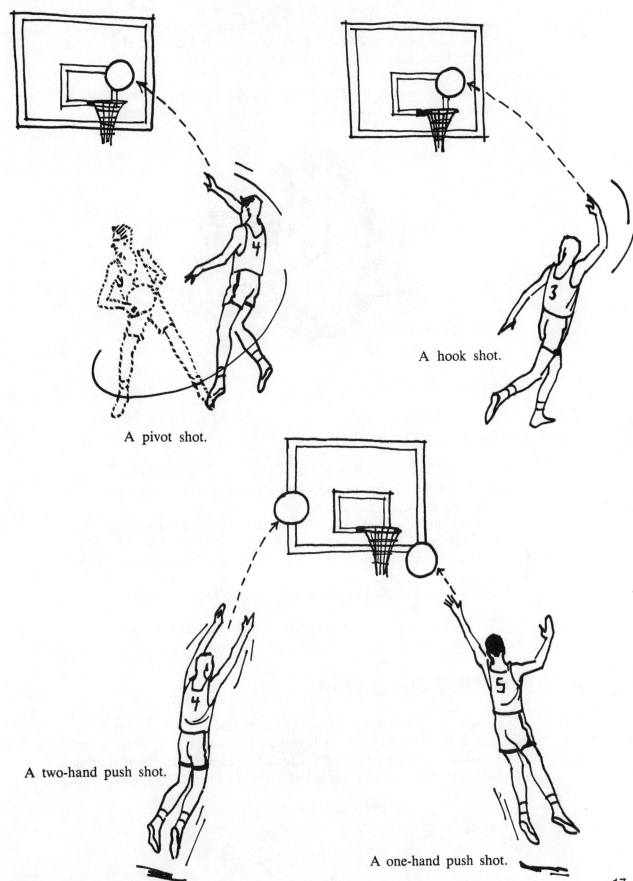

A pivot shot.

A hook shot.

A two-hand push shot.

A one-hand push shot.

SCORING

A goal is made when a live ball enters the basket from above and remains in the basket or passes through it. Each field goal counts 2 points. A goal from a free throw counts 1 point for the team into whose basket the ball is thrown.

The winning team is the one which has the greater number of points when the game ends.

EXTRA PERIODS

If the score is tied at the end of the second half, play shall continue without change of baskets for one or more extra periods with a one-minute intermission before each extra period.

For games played in halves, the length of each extra period shall be 5 minutes. In games played in quarters, the length of each extra period shall be 3 minutes. As many such periods as are necessary to break the tie shall be played.

The game ends if at the end of any extra period the score is not tied.

FORFEIT OF GAME

The referee shall forfeit the game if a team refuses to play after being instructed to do so by either official. If the team to which the game is forfeited is ahead, the score at the time of forfeiture shall stand. If this team is not ahead the score shall be recorded as 2–0 in its favor.

SUBSTITUTIONS

A substitute reports to the scorer, giving his name and number and the number of the player who is being replaced. He may enter the game only after the scorer sounds his horn and he is beckoned into the court by the official.

GAME PROCEDURE

A player must get the ball out of his team's back court and over the center line within 10 seconds of gaining possession. The Trail Official is primarily responsible for the calling of a violation of the 10-second rule.

Note how the Lead Official has moved down court in anticipation of the play there.

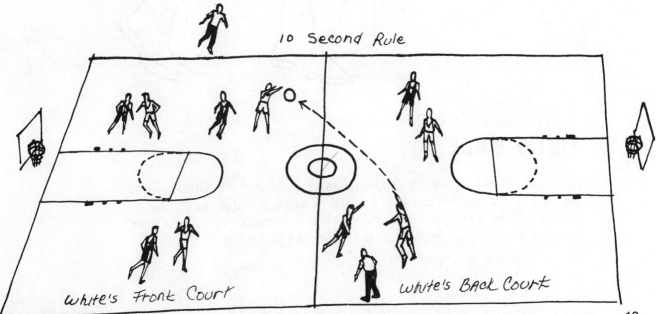

10 Second Rule

White's Front Court   White's Back Court

HELD BALL

A held ball occurs when two opponents have one or both hands so firmly on the ball that neither can gain possession without undue roughness.

Each official is responsible for the visible five-second count when a closely guarded player in the front court is holding the ball.

JUMP BALL

The ball is put in play in the *center* restraining circle with a jump between two opponents at the beginning of each period or a double foul.

After a held ball, the official puts the ball in play with a jump in the center of the *nearest* restraining circle. The jump begins when the ball leaves the official's hands. The jump ends when the tapped ball touches one of the eight non-jumpers, the floor, the basket, or the backboard.

At other times the ball is put in play by a jump ball at the center of the restraining circle which is *nearest* the spot where the ball goes out-of-bounds, a double free throw violation occurs, the ball lodges in a basket support, or the ball becomes dead when neither team is in control and no goal, infraction, or end of period is involved.

FREE THROW

A free throw is a privilege given a player to score one point by an unhindered throw for goal from within the free throw circle and behind the free throw line. It starts when the ball is given to the player at the free throw line, or is placed on the line. The ball is alive when placed at the player's disposal. A free throw ends when the ball touches the ring, backboard, the floor or a player, or when a goal has been scored.

A free throw is unsuccessful when it does not enter the hoop from above, hits the backboard without touching the rim, or falls short without either touching the rim or the backboard.

If a player is awarded two free throws, it is the responsibility of the Lead Official to secure the ball after the first free throw, made or missed, and return it to the Trail Official who will again put the ball at the disposal of the free thrower.

VIOLATIONS

A violation is a rule infraction.

A player commits a violation by:

Consuming more than five seconds in completing a throw-in.

Carrying the ball into the court on a throw-in.

Leaving the designated throw-in spot.

Touching the ball in the court before it has been touched by another player after a throw-in.

Becoming the thrower-in after an official has designated another player.

Causing the ball to go out of bounds.

Reaching through the plane of the boundary line on a throw-in. (Allowances should be made if space is limited.)

Running with the ball.

Intentionally kicking the ball.

Dribbling a second time after the first dribble has ended. (Exception: when a player has lost control of the ball because of a try for goal, a bat by an opponent, or a pass or a fumble which has been touched by another player.)

Striking the ball with the fist.

Causing the ball to pass through the basket from below.

Swinging arms or elbows excessively, even though there is no contact with an opponent.

Controlling the ball in the back court for more than 10 consecutive seconds.

Touching the ball on a field goal attempt, when the ball is on its downward flight, above the level of the ring, and in the opinion of the official has a chance to enter the basket.

Touching the basket (ring, net and appendages) when the ball is on or in the basket.

Touching the ball when it is on or in the basket or in the cylinder above.

It is not a violation if the player has his hand legally in contact with the ball and the contact continues after the ball enters the basket.

Remaining for more than 3 seconds in the free throw lane while the ball is in control of the players team in his front court. Allowances are made for the player who has dribbled in to try for a goal.

PENALTY FOR VIOLATIONS

The penalty for a violation is a throw-in by the opponents.

The ball becomes dead or remains dead when a violation occurs. The ball is awarded to a nearby opponent for a throw-in at the out-of-bounds spot nearest the violation.

If the ball passes through a basket during a dead ball period immediately following a violation, no point is scored.

The ball is then awarded to an opponent out-of-bounds at either end of that free throw line extended nearer the goal through which the ball was thrown.

The ball is handed to an opponent out-of-bounds after all violations and player control fouls.

FREE THROW VIOLATIONS

A player commits a free throw violation by:

Stepping over the free throw line while making a free throw.

Stepping over (or on) the lane boundary. (Applies to any player on either team.)

Taking more than 10 seconds to make a free throw after the ball has been placed at disposal of the shooter.

Disconcerting the player attempting the free throw.

Occupying a wrong space adjacent to the end line during a try for goal on a free throw. (Opponents of the free thrower must occupy alternate lane spaces adjacent to the end line during the try.)

After a free throw violation the ball is put in play as follows:

If the violation is by the free thrower or his teammate, no point can be scored on that throw. The ball becomes dead when the violation occurs and is put in play by any opponent who may take the ball for a throw-in to either side of the court where the free throw line extended intersects the sideline.

When the violation is by the opponent of the free thrower, and the free throw is *unsuccessful*, the ball is put in play by a substitute free throw attempted by the same free thrower.

When the violation is by the opponent of the free thrower, and the free throw is *successful*, the violation is disregarded and the goal counts. The ball is put in play again by awarding it to the opponents for a throw-in at the end line.

PERSONAL FOUL

A personal foul is a player foul which involves contact with an opponent while the ball is alive or after the ball is in possession of a player for a throw-in.

A player commits a personal foul by:

Holding an opponent.

Pushing an opponent.

Charging into an opponent.

Tripping an opponent.

Impeding the progress of an opponent by extending arm, shoulder, hip or knee or by bending the body in other than a normal position.

Making contact with ball holder from behind—a form of pushing.

Making contact caused by momentum of a player who has thrown for a goal is a form of charging.

Dribbling into the path of an opponent.

Dribbling between two opponents when the space is not adequate.

Dribbling between an opponent and the boundary line, unless the space is such as to offer a reasonable chance for him to go through without contact.

If a dribbler in his progress has established a straight line path, he may not be crowded out of that path but, if an opponent is able legally to establish a defensive position in that path, the dribbler must avoid contact by changing direction or ending his dribble.

Standing closer than a normal step behind a stationary opponent when screening.

Making contact with a stationary opponent when assuming a position alongside or in front of him.

Assuming a position so close to a moving opponent that he cannot avoid contact by stopping or changing direction.

Being in closer proximity while screening than one normal step from the opponent being screened. (The speed of the player to be screened will determine where the screener may take his stationary position.)

Moving, after assuming a screening position, in any direction except in the same direction and path as that of the opponent.

It is *not* a personal foul if a player's hand comes in contact with his opponent's hand while it is on the ball and is incidental to an attempt to play the ball.

Bonus Situation

PENALTY FOR A PERSONAL FOUL

The penalty for a personal foul is a free throw.

The Trail Official always *hands* the ball to the free thrower, whether it is the first or second free throw.

Offender is charged with one foul and if it is his fifth personal foul, or if it is flagrant, he is disqualified. The offended player is awarded free throws as follows:

1. One free throw for:
    a. A foul against a field goal thrower whose try is successful.
    b. Each foul which is a part of a multiple foul.

2. Two free throws for:
    a. A foul against a field goal thrower whose try is unsuccessful.
    b. An intentional foul.
    c. Any single flagrant foul.

3. Bonus free throw for:
    a. Each common foul (except player control) beginning with a team's seventh personal foul during the half in a game played in halves, or fifth foul during the quarter in a game played in quarters, provided the first attempt is successful.

4. No free throws for:
    a. Each common foul before the bonus rule is in effect.
    b. A double foul.
    c. A player control foul.
    d. A double foul, one or both fouls of which are flagrant or intentional.

5. In case of a false double or a false multiple foul, each foul carries its own penalty.

The specified number of free throws is awarded for each foul which is a part of a false double or a false multiple foul.

TECHNICAL FOUL

A technical foul is (a) a foul by a non player; (b) a player foul which does not involve contact with an opponent; (c) a player foul which involves unsportsmanlike contact with an opponent while the ball is dead; or (d) a player control foul which is a common foul committed by a player while he is in control.

A team, player, or nonplayer may commit a technical foul by:

Delaying game by preventing the ball from being promptly made alive.

Being unready to start the game at either half.

Failing to supply scorers with names and numbers of each squad member who may participate, 10 minutes before starting time.

Failing to provide a list of the five starting players at least 10 minutes before starting time.

Taking more than five time-outs during regulation time.

Having more than five squad members on the court at one time.

Failing to report a number change to the scorer or an official.

Participating after being disqualified.

Wearing an illegal or identical number.

Grasping the basket.

Leaving the court for an unauthorized reason.

Using unsportsmanlike tactics.

Interfering with the ball after a goal.

Using profanity.

Baiting an opponent or obstructing the vision of an opponent.

Climbing on a teammate to secure greater height to handle the ball.

Knowingly attempting a free throw to which he is not entitled.

Indicating resentment at being charged with a foul.

A team shall be prohibited from using television monitoring or replay equipment or megaphones and mechanical sounding devices at courtside for coaching purposes.

PENALTY FOR A TECHNICAL FOUL

The penalty for most technical fouls is one free throw.

When the Official administers a technical foul, no players are lined up on the free-throw lane.

After the free throw is completed following the technical foul, the ball is put in play again at mid-court.

A player may be disqualified for any one flagrant foul.

If the foul is committed by a squad member, one free throw is awarded. A second free throw is awarded if the foul is flagrant or intentional. If a foul is committed by a coach, team attendant or follower, the offended team shall be awarded two free throws. The captain shall designate the free thrower.

One free throw is awarded for each change or addition in the starting line up.

The third technical foul charged to any coach, any squad member, or any bench personnel shall be considered to be flagrant. If the offender is a coach, team attendant or follower, he shall go to his team's locker room or leave the building until the game has ended. If the offender is a player or substitute, he shall be banished from the vicinity of the court. For failure to comply, the referee may forfeit the game.

OFFICIATING

The importance of competent basketball officiating cannot be overemphasized. The game is enhanced by good officiating, but can easily be ruined by poor officiating.

It takes many years to become a proficient basketball official. The I.A.A.B.O. was founded to maintain the highest standards of basketball officiating. It now has 13,600 members in forty states, the District of Columbia, all the Canadian provinces and eleven other foreign countries. Its clinicians are available to assist young men and women interested in pursuing careers in officiating. The I.A.A.B.O. offers tests, slides, publications, clinics and a Basketball Referee School, in its ongoing effort to have available at all times an adequate number of thoroughly trained and capable officials. Those interested in basketball officiating should contact the I.A.A.B.O. Headquarters, P.O. Box 661, West Hartford, Connecticut, 06107.

Paul "Frosty" Francis, Jr.
Executive Director
International Association of
Approved Basketball Officials, Inc.

OFFICIALS

The Referee inspects and approves all equipment, including court, baskets, ball, backboards.

The Referee inspects timer's and scorer's signals.

The Referee designates the official timepiece and its operator.

The Referee designates the official scorebook and the official scorer.

The Referee is responsible for notifying each captain three minutes before each half is to begin.

The Referee checks and approves the score at the end of each half.

The Referee also:

1. Decides whether or not a goal shall count if officials disagree.
2. May forfeit the game when conditions warrant.
3. Decides upon matters on which the timers and scorers disagree.
4. Has the power to make decisions on any points not specifically covered by the rules.

Either official may penalize a player, coach, substitute, team attendant, or team follower for unsportsmanlike conduct.

Either official may call fouls on either team, or its supporters, if they act in such a way as to interfere with the proper conduct of the game. Discretion must be used by the officials.

Either official has the power to make decisions for infractions of the rules committed within or outside the boundary lines, and at any time from the beginning of play to the Referee's approval of the final score. This includes the periods when the game may be momentarily stopped for any reason.

The Referee's approval of the score book at the end of the game terminates the jurisdiction of the officials.

SCORERS AND TIMERS

The scorer(s) and timer(s) should report to the table in sufficient time to secure line-ups and check the timing equipment so that all will be in readiness when officials arrive to give them pre-game instructions on ground rules.

A single timer and a single scorer may be used, provided they are trained people and acceptable to the Referee.

I.A.A.B.O.
INSTRUCTIONS TO TIMEKEEPERS

Prepared by the Visualization and Education Committee of
the International Association of Approved Basketball Officials

ROUTINE

1. Check time with Western Union to see that both coaches have the official time. This should be done thirty (30) minutes before game time.
2. Review with Officials signals for time-out, time-in, foul and violation.
3. Keep eyes on Officials throughout the game.
4. Check on the duration of time-outs, substitutions, time of periods, etc.
5. Note the position of ball, when you signal end of any period or extra period. Timers should never indicate goals scored or fouls made unless the Referee so requests.
6. Check on duration of time between 1st and 2nd, 3rd and 4th periods, and between halves. At least three minutes before the beginning of each half notify the Referee so that the teams may be informed of the starting time.
7. Seek designation from Referee as to which is Official Timepiece and its Operator.
8. It is strongly recommended that the Operator of the Official Timepiece be an Adult.
9. When an electric timepiece is used, have a manual clock on hand in the event of failure of the electric clock.
10. It is recommended that the Official Timer have the use of a starter's gun to indicate the end of a period.
11. Sounding of scorer's signal does not cause Official Timepiece to be stopped.

START CLOCK (Official should indicate this by a chopping motion of his hand.)

1. When ball is legally tapped on all jump balls. (Chopping motion by non-tossing Official)
2. When the ball has touched a player in the court, if resumption of play is by a throw-in after clock has been stopped. (Chopping motion)
3. When ball is legally touched after a missed free throw and ball is to remain alive. (Chopping motion trail official)
4. In case signal is not given to start the clock, clock should be started unless Official specifically signals that time should remain out.

STOP CLOCK

1. When time expires at the end of any period.
2. When an Official gives a time-out signal. The Official will give a time-out signal when:
   a. Foul is called by holding his hand with fingers closed at arm's length above his head.
   b. Jump ball is declared by holding his thumbs up at shoulder height away from body and motioning upward with both arms extended.
   c. Violation occurs by holding his hand with fingers extended at arm's length above his head.
3. When an Official orders time-out:
   a. To avoid unusual delay.
   b. To repair or adjust equipment.
   c. For an injury or other emergency.
   d. Upon request of a player whose team has player control or when ball is dead.

GENERAL

Referee shall appoint the Official Timer as operator of the Official Timepiece. Second timer should assume responsibilities of operating time-out watch and checking Official Timepiece.

If timekeeper's signal is not heard the timekeeper shall go on the court and notify the Official noting the position of the ball when time expires.

Timer shall sound a warning signal 15 seconds before the end of an intermission, a charged time-out or a time-out for replacing a disqualified player.

Notify scorers ten minutes prior to starting time.

LENGTH OF PERIODS

High School Games—8 minute quarters; 1 minute between quarters and extra periods and 10 minutes between halves; extra periods, 3 minutes.

College Games—Two 20 minute halves and 15 minutes between halves, 1 minute between extra periods; extra periods, 5 minutes.

All Games—Time-outs requested by players are for 1 minute. Time-outs to replace disqualified players are for 1 minute. Time-outs for substitutions for injuries are not charged.

(As a general rule the Official Timepiece should be stopped every time an Official blows his whistle.)

I.A.A.B.O.
INSTRUCTIONS TO SCORERS

Prepared by the Visualization and Education Committee of
the International Association of Approved Basketball Officials

1. Seek designation from Referee as to who is the official scorer and which is official scorebook and consult with him as to signals used to designate fouls and time-outs. The official scorer should wear black and white striped garment.
2. Obtain names and numbers of all players who may participate in the game at least ten (10) minutes before the scheduled start of the game. At least ten (10) minutes before scheduled starting time, have each team designate its five starting players. Report any failure to comply to the referee.
3. Record field goals made, free throws made and missed, running summary of points scored, personal and technical fouls on each player, team personal fouls per half and time outs.
4. Designate each goal and each foul thusly:

Field goal	2 Two shot foul	OO
Free throw attempt	O Bonus opportunity	O+O
Free throw made	⊕ Personal Foul	P1 P2 P3 P4 P5
	Technical Foul	T1 T2 T3

Field goals scored in wrong basket are not credited to any player but are credited to the team in a footnote. Points awarded for illegally touching ball or baskets are credited to the thrower. When a live ball goes in a basket, the last player who touched it causes it to go there.

5. Notify official (a) when team has taken the legal five time-outs, (b) when a player has had five personal fouls, (c) after a team has been charged with six personal fouls in either half of a game played in halves or four in a game played in quarters, (d) when a team has used time-outs in excess of the five legal. In (b), (c) and (d) if play is in progress at time of discovery, withhold whistle until ball is dead or in control of offending team, (e) when ball is dead or in control of team of offending player if player is discovered who has not reported to scorer or who has changed his number without reporting it, or who is illegally in the game, (f) player enters while wearing illegal number, (g) when ball is dead and the clock is stopped, if coach requests that a correctable error be prevented or rectified.
6. Check with fellow scorer on each entry in score book, such as score, fouls, substitutions, charged time-outs, etc. If any discrepancy occurs notify referee at once on next dead ball—time-out situation.
7. Blow horn to stop game only when ball is dead and time is out.
8. When a substitute reports (must be ready and entitled to enter game), signal when ball is dead and time is out and before change of status of ball is about to occur. Substitute must give his number and number of player he is replacing. Allow substitute to go on court only when official beckons. Do not signal after ball has been placed at the disposal of a free thrower. If ball is dead after a free throw attempt, a substitution may be made. If thrower is to be replaced, be sure that it is legal for another player to attempt that particular throw. A substitute cannot replace a player designated to jump or designated to attempt a free throw. He must wait until the next dead ball, time-out situation.
9. A player who has been withdrawn may not reenter before the next opportunity to substitute after the clock has started following his replacement.
10. Substitutions between halves shall be made to the scorer prior to the signal which ends the intermission.
11. Either official scorer or a delegated assistant must be at the scorers' table with the official scorebook at all times, including the half-time intermission.
12. Scorer shall have a bonus-throw indicator.
13. No free throws are awarded for: (1) each common foul before the bonus rule is in effect; (2) a player control foul; (3) a double foul; or (4) a double foul, one or both of which are flagrant. Fouls are to be recorded against the player or players committing the fouls.

Scorebook of home team is the official book, unless referee rules otherwise.

Scorebook should remain at scorers' table during intermissions.

Scorers should be adults when possible. They should be equipped with a sounding device unlike that used by the Officials or Timers to signal the Officials.

OFFICIAL BASKETBALL SIGNALS

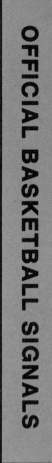
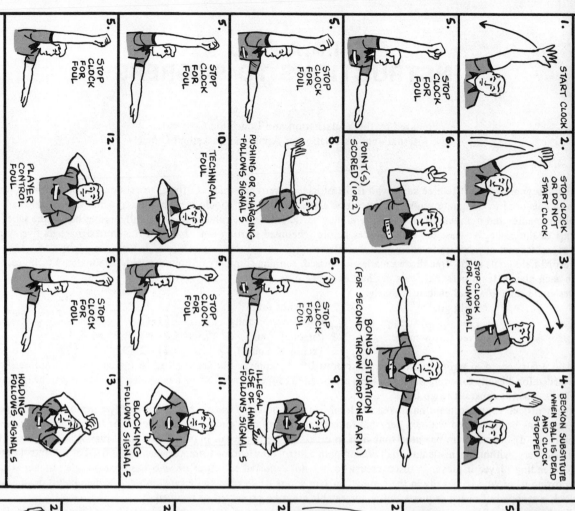

1. START CLOCK

2. STOP CLOCK OR DO NOT START CLOCK

3. STOP CLOCK FOR JUMP BALL

4. BECKON SUBSTITUTE WHEN BALL IS DEAD AND CLOCK STOPPED

5. STOP CLOCK FOR FOUL

6. POINT(S) SCORED (1 OR 2)

7. BONUS SITUATION (FOR SECOND THROW DROP ONE ARM)

8. PUSHING OR CHARGING -FOLLOWS SIGNAL 5

9. ILLEGAL USE OF HAND -FOLLOWS SIGNAL 5

10. TECHNICAL FOUL

11. BLOCKING -FOLLOWS SIGNAL 5

12. PLAYER CONTROL FOUL

13. HOLDING FOLLOWS SIGNAL 5

FOR FREE THROW VIOLATION: USE SIGNALS 2 AND 18.

FOR BASKET INTERFERENCE: USE SIGNALS 16 OR 14 AND 6.

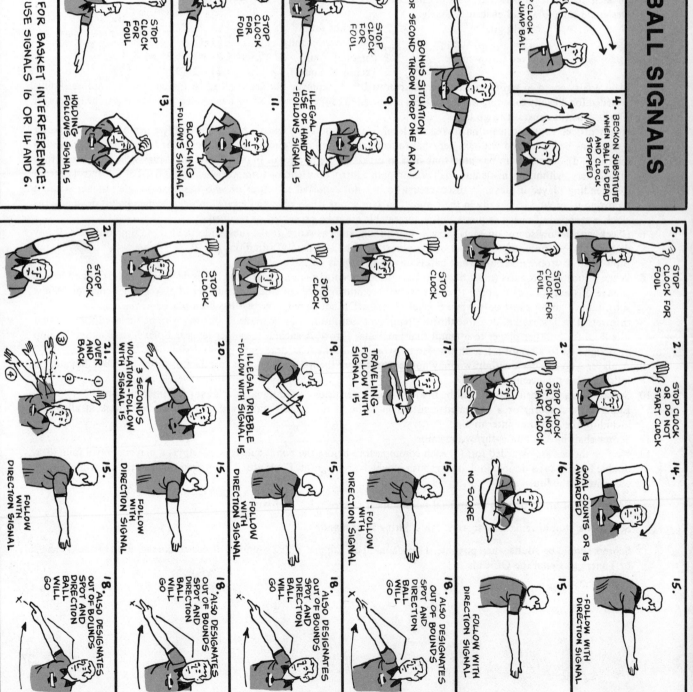

2. STOP CLOCK

2. STOP CLOCK

2. STOP CLOCK

2. STOP CLOCK

5. STOP CLOCK FOR FOUL

5. STOP CLOCK FOR FOUL

14. GOAL COUNTS OR IS AWARDED

2. STOP CLOCK OR DO NOT START CLOCK

2. STOP CLOCK OR DO NOT START CLOCK

21. OVER AND BACK VIOLATION-FOLLOW WITH SIGNAL 15

20. 3 SECONDS VIOLATION-FOLLOW WITH SIGNAL 15

19. ILLEGAL DRIBBLE -FOLLOW WITH SIGNAL 15

17. TRAVELING- FOLLOW WITH SIGNAL 15

16. NO SCORE

15. FOLLOW WITH DIRECTION SIGNAL

15. FOLLOW WITH DIRECTION SIGNAL

15. FOLLOW WITH DIRECTION SIGNAL

15. FOLLOW WITH DIRECTION SIGNAL

15. -FOLLOW WITH DIRECTION SIGNAL

15. FOLLOW WITH DIRECTION SIGNAL

15. -FOLLOW WITH DIRECTION SIGNAL

18. FOLLOW WITH DIRECTION SIGNAL BALL WILL GO

18. ALSO DESIGNATES OUT OF BOUNDS SPOT AND DIRECTION BALL WILL GO

18. ALSO DESIGNATES OUT OF BOUNDS SPOT AND DIRECTION BALL WILL GO

18. ALSO DESIGNATES OUT OF BOUNDS SPOT AND DIRECTION BALL WILL GO

18. ALSO DESIGNATES OUT OF BOUNDS SPOT AND DIRECTION BALL WILL GO

BENCH BEHAVIOR

Officials are expected to penalize the conduct of the coach and others on the bench if it is not in conformity with the rules. The coach is required to remain on the bench except for certain listed situations.

FLOOR COVERAGE (FRONT COURT)

The Lead Official pays particular attention to the play in the front court. The Trail Official moves on to the court in order to see the play better, always being careful not to interfere with the play or players. It is the Trail Official who is responsible for all violations regarding the division line and it is the Trail Official who calls the 10-second play in the back court.

PROCEDURE IN SUBSTITUTION

When a substitute enters the game, he may be beckoned in by either of the two officials. The official nearer the table usually signals the substitute to enter.

POSITION OF OFFICIALS
DURING TIME-OUT PERIOD

Official with the ball takes the position where play will be resumed. His fellow official stations himself just on the court facing the scoring table, and is available when help is needed.

THROW–IN (STARTING THE CLOCK)

The Trail Official—the official here responsible for the signal to start the clock—has completed his chopping motion as the ball touches a player in-bounds.

The Trail Official hands (never tosses) the ball to the player out of bounds. He will give the silent count of five seconds allowed for the throw-in. The Trail Official has his hand up, ready to bring it down in a chopping motion as soon as the ball touches a player on the court. The timer watches for this signal to start the clock.

COURT COVERAGE (LEAD OFFICIAL)

Since the ball has moved near the side line, the official shifts to the corner to have a complete view of the situation near the side line. The Lead Official must be quick and alert in order to follow the play from the best viewing spot.

COURT COVERAGE (TRAIL OFFICIAL)

The Trail Official moves to a position from which he can observe the flight of the ball. He must be able to see if it passes over the top of the backboard, or if it strikes the supports. The Trail Official is primarily responsible for the action in the back half of the front court.

Both officials move with the action, taking up positions which give them the clearest and most advantageous view.

COURT COVERAGE (LEAD OFFICIAL)

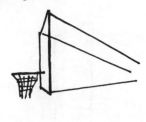

The Lead Official watches the front half of the front court. He is responsible for calling an infraction of the 3-second rule, as well as fouls and violations in this area. The Lead Official pays little attention to the flight of the ball as he is not looking above eye level.

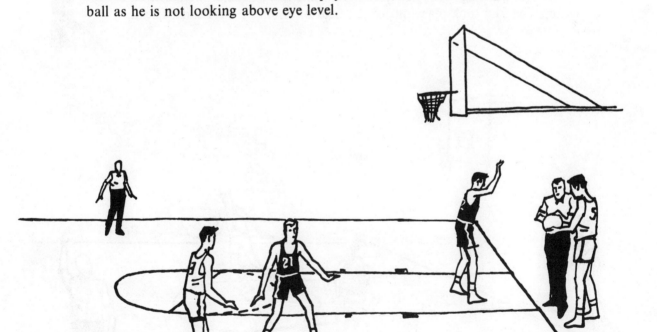

When the ball goes out-of-bounds under the basket, the Lead Official hands the ball to the thrower-in on the nearer free throw lane line extended. The ball is also taken to the nearer free throw lane extended if the throw-in spot is behind the backboard.

COURT COVERAGE (HEAD—TRAIL)

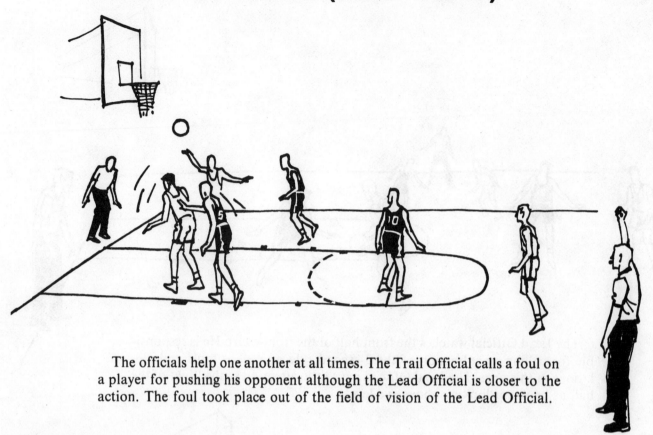

The officials help one another at all times. The Trail Official calls a foul on a player for pushing his opponent although the Lead Official is closer to the action. The foul took place out of the field of vision of the Lead Official.

After a goal has been awarded for basket interference or goal tending, the ball is given to the thrower-in to restart the game.

FLOOR PATTERNS
OFFENSE AND DEFENSE
by
BRUCE BASSETT

Former Athletic Director, International House
New York, N.Y.

OUT-OF-BOUNDS PLAY UNDER THE BASKET

X-1 screens for X-2 who cuts toward the basket, "picking off" the man guarding him, O-2, on the screen set by X-1.

O-1   X-2   X-1   O-2

If O-1, the man guarding X-1, switches defensive assignments with O-2 and picks up X-2 when he cuts off the screen set by X-1, the pass to X-2 in the preceding diagram will be ineffective. However, if O-1 switches, X-1 is left without a defensive man between him and the basket. If X-1 rolls off the screen he has set and cuts for the basket, he will be free for an easy shot.

OUT-OF-BOUNDS PLAY
FROM SIDELINES

X-2, the center, breaks upcourt and receives a pass from X-1, who is throwing in from out of bounds. X-3, the forward, has come up and set a screen on O, the man guarding X-1. After passing to X-2, X-1 cuts quickly toward the basket, picking off his defensive man on X-3's screen. X-2 gives X-1 a return pass and X-1 has a clear path to the basket. There are any number of possible out-of-bounds plays; most of them utilize a pass and a cut toward the basket.

BASIC FOOTWORK OF FORWARD PLAY

To receive a pass from the guard on his side of the floor, the forward should draw his defense man in toward the center of the floor and then break out toward the pass.

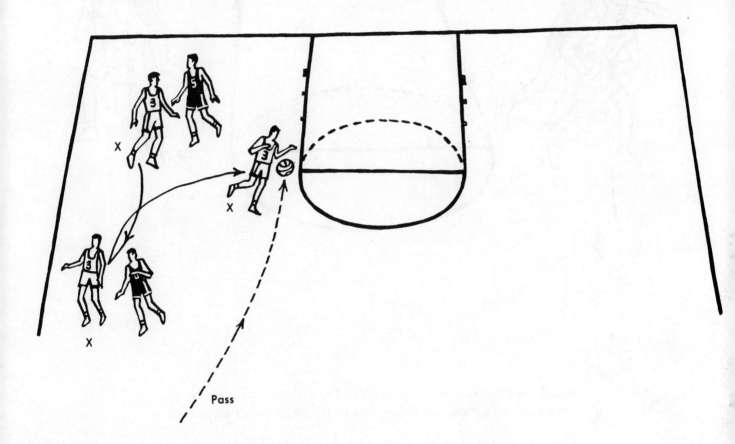

Pass

If the man guarding the forward overplays him by tending to play between the guard and the forward (in an attempt to prevent a pass from the guard to the forward) rather than between the forward and the basket, the forward can line his defense man up and then cut behind him for a pass and a clear path to the basket.

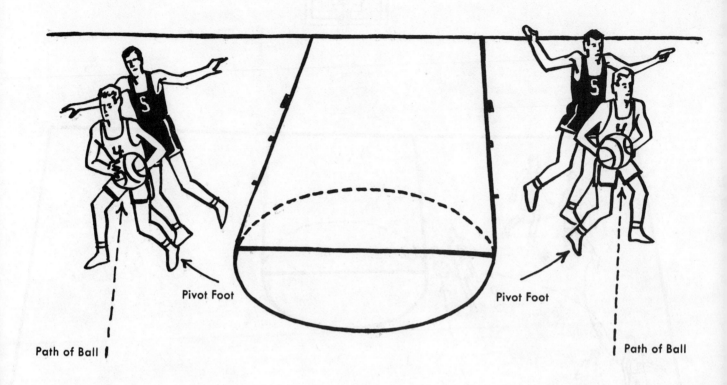

Path of Ball

Pivot Foot

Pivot Foot

Path of Ball

When the forward breaks up court and receives a pass from the guard he should use the foot nearest the middle of the court as his pivot foot.

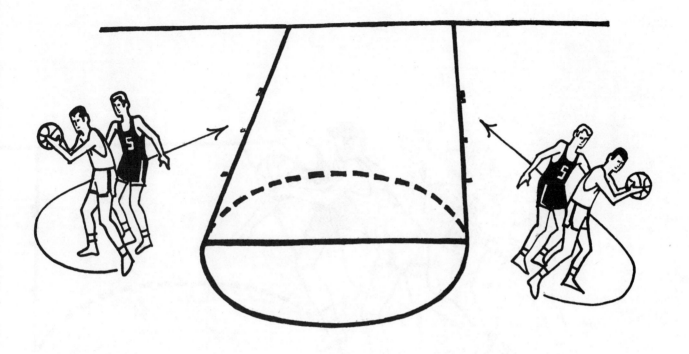

When the forward receives the pass from the guard, his back is toward the end line. Upon receiving the pass the forward has several options: If the defense man guarding the forward is not too close to him, the forward can shoot; if the defense man is playing the forward very tightly, the forward can pivot in the direction of the side line, pinning his defense man behind him, and drive toward the basket for a shot.

The pivot and drive toward the basket is made more effective if the forward is able to lure the defense man toward the center of the court and closer to him; then when the forward pivots in the direction of the side line and drives toward the basket, he will have the defensive man in a better position for pinning him behind the pivot. A pivot and feint toward the center of the court is conducive to putting the defensive man in this position.

The forward then pivots in the opposite direction.
This defensive man is pinned behind and a clear path to the basket is open.

ZONE DEFENSE

In a zone defense a team defends by assigning its men to be responsible for certain areas of the court rather than to certain men on the other team. Where a defensive man positions himself in the area depends upon where the ball is at the time. There are many types of zone defenses—that is, there are many ways that the court area around the basket being defended can be allocated. There are even defenses which combine a man-to-man defense with a zone defense.

Some of the basic zone defenses are:

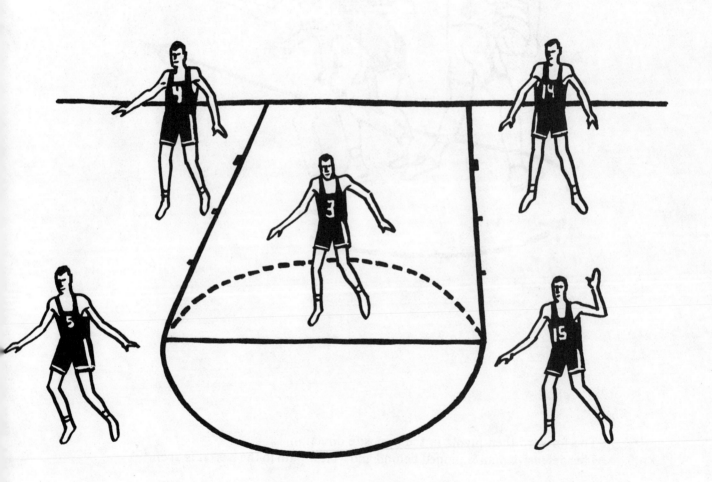

THE 2—1—2 ZONE

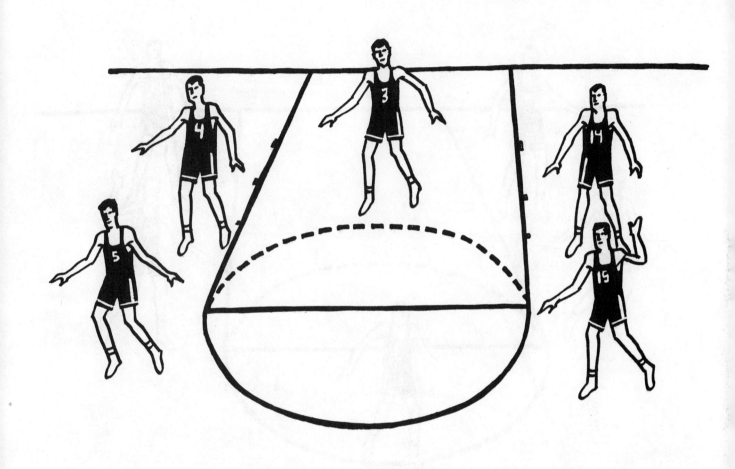

THE 2—2—1 ZONE

THE 1—2—2 ZONE

THE 1—3—1 ZONE

The area assigned to each of the players in a zone depends on the type of zone used and on the desires of the coach, which are influenced by such factors as height and speed of each player and the offensive abilities of the other team. Generally, the areas are assigned so that whenever the ball is on the periphery of the zone, there will be three defensive men in the line of the ball and the basket.

Taking the 2 - 1 - 2 zone as an example:

* * *

The shaded area is considered the end of the area in which the other team can pose an offensive threat and the area in which the zone defense can be effectively maintained. No player on the defensive team may go outside this area to defend. This limitation is set by the coach, just as is that of each of the sub-areas within the shaded area where each defensive player may move.

* * *

The offensive team usually attempts to break the zone defense by passing the ball quickly around the periphery until the defense has not shifted quickly enough to keep up with the ball and a free shot is open.

ZONE SHIFT

Example of how a 2 - 1 - 2 zone might shift with the movement of the ball.

The defense shifts as the ball is moved around the periphery of the zone and tries to keep the zone impenetrable. This forces the offensive team to shoot from outside the zone where the accuracy is generally less and gives the defensive team playing the zone more men grouped near the basket to gather the rebounds from missed shots.

SAMPLE OFFENSIVE PLAY AGAINST
MAN-TO-MAN DEFENSE

The guard with the ball, in this case X-1, drives into the middle until he is effectively checked by his defensive man or until he reaches the free-throw line.

Then X-1 turns his back to the basket and looks for X-2, who has faked as if to cut toward the corner and has timed his cut to coincide with X-1's turn toward him. At this point there are several options:

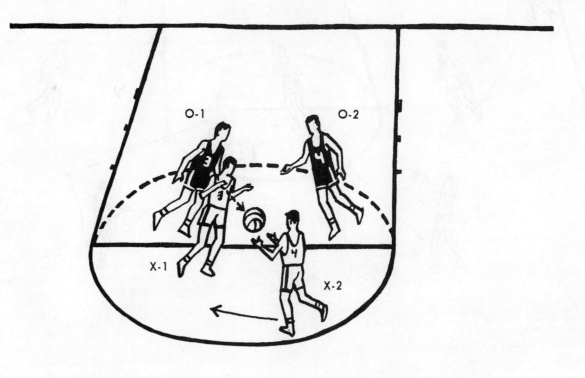

If X-1 passes the ball to X-2, X-2 may take a set shot if his defensive man, O-2, has dropped behind X-1. However, if either O-1 or O-2 attempts to get around X-1 to guard X-2, X-2 can drive on the other side of X-1. X-1 can also roll toward the basket and the defense will be left with one defensive man trying to guard two offensive men. If the remaining defensive man, O-1, picks up X-2 as he drives toward the basket, X-1 is open for a pass and an easy shot; if O-1 does not pick up X-2, X-2 has a clear path to the basket.

If a defensive man comes out to guard X-2 from the other side of X-1, then the situation is just reversed, and X-2 drives to his right past X-1.

* * *

O-1 must decide whether to guard X-1 or X-2; whichever one he guards, the other is left free. O-2 is screened by X-1 when he tries to follow X-2's drive; both X-1 and X-2 are ahead of him.

As another alternative, X-1 can maintain his dribble when he turns after dribbling into the middle, let X-2 cut by him, and then drive off of X-2. This usually gives X-1 clearance for a short shot, but care must be taken that the violation of a moving screen is not committed. Basically, these are the alternatives from which the two guards can choose their play. Of course, the effectiveness of these maneuvers can be heightened by some added feints and options. When the guards X-1 and X-2 become more familiar with their options, their moves will be aimed primarily at taking advantage of what the defense does.

For example, if O-2 guarding X-2 anticipates the pass from X-1 to X-2, then X-2 can fake a cut behind X-1 and then cut straight for the basket and the pass from X-1. Note how O-2 overplays X-2 in anticipation of a cut behind X-1.

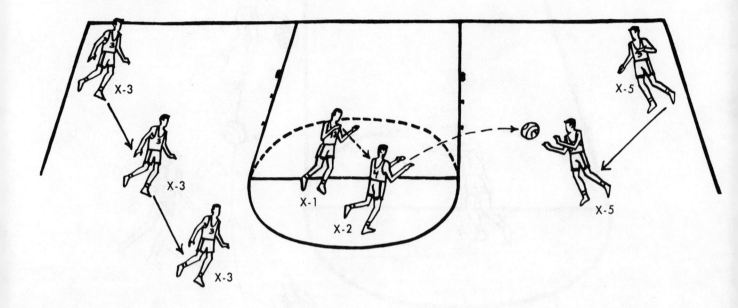

Assuming that X-1 and X-2 do not use their options, the pattern continues, bringing into play the forwards who have broken out of the corners. X-2 upon receiving the pass from X-1 has an option of passing either to X-3 or X-5.

Assuming X-2 passes to X-5, the opposite forward, X-3, should come out further for defensive purposes. The offensive team must always have men back far enough to provide a defense if the defensive team should suddenly obtain the ball.

Upon passing the ball to X-5, X-2 cuts toward the basket and X-5 has several options. He may shoot if he is open, he may pass back to X-2 who is cutting toward the basket, he may drive toward the basket, or he may drive toward the center of the floor. Whatever happens, X-1 must drop back for defensive purposes as soon as X-2 has cut by him.

* * *

If X-5 does not exercise another option he drives across the court.

No defense players are shown.

In driving across the court, X-5 may find freedom to shoot. If not, he can stop and turn his back to the basket in approximately the same position as X-1 did at the beginning of the pattern. Meanwhile, X-1 has drifted out toward the center as if solely for defensive purposes should there be a sudden turnover of the ball to the defensive team. In fact, both O-3 and O-1 will be lulled into thinking that their men, X-3 and X-1, are out of the play and as a consequence they will relax. When X-5 turns in his dribble across the court, X-1 who has been drifting out should suddenly turn and cut toward the basket. O-1 will probably be left behind by X-1's sudden reversal. X-2, who has cut to the basket, must continue moving and come back out, both to free the middle of the court and also for defensive purposes.

Note that X-1 and X-5 have options similar to the ones X-1 and X-2 had when they crossed at the beginning of the pattern. However, these would only be utilized if O-1 is not left behind by X-1's sudden reversal and cut toward the basket. Of course, upon passing off to X-1, X-5 should also roll toward the basket, leaving O-1 behind him and making O-5 choose between guarding X-1 or X-5.

If O-1 is not left behind, X-1 will cut by X-5 so as to run O-1 into the screen of X-5.

If O-3 turns his head from X-3 or relaxes because the play is occurring behind him, X-3 can cut for the basket and receive a pass from X-5.

Whenever X-1 or X-2, the guards, cut through to the basket, they must come right back out so as to keep the middle open and to be ready to change to defense if the other team gets the ball and starts toward its basket.

* * *

Throughout this sequence of options, the center, X-4, must roam along the back line so as to keep himself and his defensive man O-4 out of the way and yet be available for a pass and in good position to take a rebound after any shot. Where this position is depends on many factors of varying importance. Some of these factors are where the ball is, what options are likely to be used, where the rest of the team is positioned, and where the man guarding him is.

**PROPER FREE THROW
SHOT PROCEDURE**

BASKETBALL RULES

Official Rules printed by special permission of the National Collegiate Athletic Association.

RULE 4—DEFINITIONS

Basket
SECTION 1. A basket is the 18-inch [45.72cm] ring, its flange and braces, and appended net through which players attempt to throw the ball. A team's own basket is the one into which its players try to throw the ball. The visiting team shall have the irrevocable choice of baskets at which it may practice before the game and this basket shall be its choice for the first half. The teams shall change baskets for the second half.

Blocking
SECTION 2. Blocking is illegal personal contact which impedes the progress of an opponent.

Bonus Free Throw
SECTION 3. A bonus free throw is a second free throw which is awarded for each common foul (except a player control foul) committed by a player of a team beginning with that team's seventh personal foul in a half of a game played in halves, provided the first free throw for the foul is successful.

Boundary Lines
SECTION 4. Boundary lines of the court consist of end and side lines. The inside edges of these lines define the in-bounds and out-of-bounds areas.

Change of Status
SECTION 5. Change of status is the time at which a dead ball becomes alive or a live ball becomes dead.

Change of status is about to occur when:
a. A player has started to make a throw-in.
b. 80% of the time limit count has expired.
c. An official is ready to make the toss for a jump.
d. An official starts to place the ball at the disposal of a free thrower.

In Control—Player, Team
SECTION 6. a. A player is in control when he is holding a live ball or dribbling it.

b. A team is in control when a player of the team is in control and also while a live ball is being passed between teammates. Team control continues until: the ball is in flight during a try for goal; or an opponent secures control; or the ball becomes dead. There is no team control: during a jump ball; a throw-in; during the tapping of a rebound; or after the ball is in flight during a try for goal. In these situations, team control is reestablished when a player secures control.

Disqualified Player
SECTION 7. A disqualified player is one who is barred from further participation in the game because of committing his fifth personal foul, or a flagrant foul, or for infraction of Rule 10-6a or b.

Dribble
SECTION 8. A dribble is ball movement caused by a player in control who bats, pushes, or taps the ball to the floor once or several times. During a dribble the ball may be batted into the air, provided it is permitted to strike the floor one or more times before the ball is touched again.

The dribble may be started by:
a. Batting, tapping or throwing the ball into the air.
b. Batting, pushing or tapping the ball to the floor.

The dribble ends when:
a. The dribbler catches the ball with one or both hands.
b. The dribbler touches the ball with both hands simultaneously.
c. The dribbler is unable to immediately catch or continue to dribble the ball.
d. An opponent bats the ball.
e. The ball becomes dead.

QUESTION [1]—Is a player dribbling while tapping the ball during a jump, or when a pass rebounds from his hand, or when he fumbles, or when he taps a rebound or a pass away from other players who are attempting to get it? ANSWER—No. The player is not in control under these conditions.

QUESTION [2]—Is it a dribble when a player stands still and: (a) bounces the ball; or (b) holds the ball and touches it on the floor once or more? ANSWER—(a)Yes. (b) No.

QUESTION [3]—May a dribbler alternate hands? **ANSWER**—Yes.

QUESTION [4]—Prior to beginning or after completing the dribble. A¹ tosses the ball, one or several times, from hand to hand? **ANSWER**—Legal. The act of tossing the ball from one hand to another is administered exactly as if A¹ were holding the ball. Foot movement limitations are identical for a player holding the ball and for tossing it from one hand to the other.

Dunking
SECTION 9. Dunking (or stuffing) is the driving, or forcing, or pushing, or attempting to force a ball through the basket with the hand(s).

Extra Period
SECTION 10. Extra period is the extension of playing time necessary to break a tie score.

Foul
SECTION 11. A foul is an infraction of the rules that is charged and penalized.

a. A **common foul** is a personal foul which is neither flagrant nor intentional nor committed against a player trying for field goal, nor a part of a double or multiple foul.

b. A **double foul** is a situation in which two opponents commit personal fouls against each other at approximately the same time. A false double foul is a situation in which there are fouls by both teams, the second of which occurs before the clock is started following the first, but such that at least one of the attributes of a double foul is absent.

c. A **flagrant foul** is an unsportsmanlike act and may be a personal or technical foul of a violent or savage nature, or a technical noncontact foul, which displays vulgar or abusive conduct. It may or may not be intentional.

d. An **intentional foul** is a personal or technical foul, which in the judgment of the official appears to be designed or premeditated. It is not based on severity of the act.

e. A **multiple foul** is a situation in which two or more teammates commit personal fouls against the same opponent at approximately the same time. A false multiple foul is a situation in which there are two or more fouls by the same team and such that the last foul is committed before the clock is started following the first, and such that at least one of the attributes of a multiple foul is absent.

f. A **personal foul** (10-11) is a player foul which involves contact with an opponent while the ball is alive or after the ball is in possession of a player for a throw-in.

g. A **player control foul** is a common foul committed by a player while he is in control.

h. A **technical foul** (10-1 through 10) is: a foul by a non-player, or a player foul which does not involve contact with an opponent, or a player foul which involves unsportsmanlike contact with an opponent while the ball is dead, except as indicated in last clause of (g) above.

i. An **unsportsmanlike foul** is a technical foul which consists of unfair, unethical or dishonorable conduct.

Free Throw
SECTION 12. A free throw is the privilege given a player to score one point by an unhindered try for goal from within the free throw circle and behind the free throw line. A free throw starts when the ball is given to the free thrower at the free throw line or is placed on the line. It ends when: the try is successful; or it is certain the try will not be successful; or when the try touches the floor or any player; or when the ball becomes dead.

Frontcourt And Backcourt
SECTION 13. a. A team's frontcourt consists of that part of the court between its end line and the nearer edge of the division line and including its basket and the in-bounds part of its backboard.

b. A team's backcourt consists of the rest of the court including its opponent's basket and in-bounds part of the backboard and the entire division line.

c. A team's midcourt is that part of its frontcourt between the division line and a parallel imaginary line 28 feet [8.53m] from the inside edge of the end boundary to the nearer edge of the midcourt area marker. This imaginary line is located by two three-foot [0.91m] lines two inches [5.08cm] wide measured from the inside edge of each side boundary and drawn at right angles to it.

d. A team's forecourt extends from the nearer edge of the midcourt area marker to the inside edge of the end boundary.

e. A live ball is in the front- or backcourt of the team in control as follows:

> 1. A ball which is in contact with a player or with the court is in the backcourt if either the ball or the player (either player if the ball is touching more than one) is touching the backcourt. It is in the frontcourt if neither the ball nor the player is touching the backcourt.

> 2. A ball which is not in contact with a player or the court retains the same status as when it was last in contact with a player or the court.

QUESTION—From the frontcourt, A passes the ball across the division line. It touches a teammate who is in the air after leaping from the backcourt or it touches an official in the backcourt. Is the ball in the backcourt? **ANSWER**—Yes. See 4-19.

Fumble

SECTION 14. A fumble is the accidental loss of player control by unintentionally dropping the ball or permitting it to slip from one's grasp.

Held Ball

SECTION 15. Held ball occurs when:

a. Opponents have hands so firmly on the ball that control cannot be obtained without undue roughness.

b. A team in its frontcourt controls the ball for five seconds in an area enclosed by screening teammates.

c. A closely guarded player, in his midcourt, dribbles, or combines dribbling and holding the ball for five seconds.

d. A closely guarded player anywhere in his frontcourt holds or dribbles the ball for five seconds.

Exceptions to (c) and (d):

1. When a player dribbles from the MIDCOURT into the forecourt, a new five-second count shall begin.

2. When a player starts a dribble in the FORECOURT, a new five-second count shall begin if the player ends the dribble anywhere in the frontcourt and then holds the ball.

The player in control is closely guarded when his opponent is in a guarding stance at a distance not exceeding six feet [1.83m] from him.

QUESTION —Is it a held ball merely because the player holding the ball is lying or sitting on the floor? **ANSWER**—No.

Holding

SECTION 16. Holding is personal contact with an opponent which interferes with his freedom of movement.

Jump Ball

SECTION 17. A jump ball is a method of putting the ball into play by tossing it up between two opponents in one of the three circles. It begins when the ball leaves the official's hand, and ends as outlined in Rule 6-4.

Lack of Action

SECTION 18. Lack of sufficient action is the failure of the responsible team to force play as required by the Comments on the Rules.

Location of a Player

SECTION 19. The location of a player (or nonplayer) is determined by where he is touching the floor as far as being in bounds or out of bounds or being in the frontcourt or backcourt is concerned. When he is in the air from a leap, his status with reference to these two factors is the same as at the time he was last in contact with the floor or an extension of the floor such as a bleacher. When the ball touches an official, it is the same as touching the floor at the official's location.

Multiple Throw

SECTION 20. A multiple throw is a succession of free throws attempted by the same team.

Pass

SECTION 21. A pass is movement of the ball caused by a player, who throws, bats or rolls the ball to another player.

Penalty

SECTION 22. A penalty for a foul is the charging of the offender with the foul and awarding one or more free throws, or awarding the ball to the opponents for a throw-in. The penalty for a violation is the awarding of the ball to the opponents for a throw-in or one or more points or a substitute free throw.

Pivot

SECTION 23. A pivot takes place when a player who is holding the ball steps once or more than once in any direction with the same foot, the other foot, called the pivot foot, being kept at its point of contact with the floor.

Rule

SECTION 24. A rule is one of the groups of laws which govern the game. A game law (commonly called a rule) sometimes states or implies the ball is dead or a foul or violation is involved. If it does not, it is assumed the ball is alive and no foul or violation has occurred to affect the given situation. A single infraction is not complicated by a second infraction unless so stated or implied.

Traveling

SECTION 25. Running with the ball (traveling) is moving a foot or the feet in any direction in excess of prescribed limits while holding the ball. The limits follow:

Item 1. A player who receives the ball while standing still may pivot, using either foot as the pivot foot.

Item 2. A player, who receives the ball while his feet are moving or who is dribbling, may stop as follows:

a. If he catches the ball while both feet are off the floor and:

1. He alights with both feet touching the floor si-

multaneously, he may pivot using either foot as the pivot foot; or

    2. He alights with first one foot touching the floor followed by the other, he may pivot using the first foot to touch the floor as the pivot foot; or

    3. He alights on one foot, he may jump off that foot and alight with both feet simultaneously, but he may not pivot before releasing the ball.

b. If he catches the ball while only one foot is off the floor:

    1. He may step with the foot which is off the floor and may then pivot using the other foot as the pivot foot; or

    2. He may jump with the foot which is on the floor and alight with both feet simultaneously, but he may not pivot before releasing the ball.

Item 3. After a player has come to a stop, he may pass or throw for goal under the following conditions:

a. In Items 1, 2a(1), 2a(2), and 2b(1), he may lift either foot, but if he lifts his pivot foot or jumps before he passes or throws for goal, the ball must leave his hand before the pivot foot again touches the floor; or if he has jumped before either foot touches the floor.

b. In Items 2a(3) and 2b(2), he may lift either foot or jump before he passes or throws for goal. However, the ball must leave his hand before a foot which has left the floor retouches it.

Item 4. A player who receives the ball as in Item 1 or a player, who comes to a stop after he receives the ball while he is moving his feet, may start a dribble under the following conditions:

a. In Items 1, 2a(1), 2a(2), and 2b(1), the ball must leave his hand before the pivot foot leaves the floor.

b. In Items 2a(3) and 2b(2), the ball must leave his hand before either foot leaves the floor.

QUESTION [1]—Is it traveling if a player falls to the floor while holding the ball? ANSWER—No, unless he makes progress by sliding.

QUESTION [2]—A[1] gains control of the ball while on the floor and then rolls or slides, after which he passes to A[2] before getting to his feet. ANSWER—Legal, unless A[1] gains an advantage when he rolls or slides.

QUESTION [3]—A[1] jumps to throw the ball. B[1] prevents the throw by placing one or both hands firmly on the ball so that: (a) A[1]; or (b) A[1] and B[1] both return to the floor holding it. ANSWER—Held ball. However, if A[1] voluntarily drops the ball before he returns to the floor and he then touches the ball before it is touched by another player, A[1] has committed a traveling violation.

Screen

SECTION 26. A screen is legal action by a player who, without causing contact, delays or prevents an opponent from reaching a desired position.

Tap

SECTION 27. A tap (tip) is the striking or batting of the ball by any part of the hand(s) while there is not player control by the tapper. The tap starts when the ball has left the player's hand(s). The tap ends in exactly the same manner as does a try (see 4-29a).

Throw-In

SECTION 28. A throw-in is a method of putting the ball in play from out of bounds in accordance with Rule 7. The throw-in begins when the ball is at the disposal of the player or team entitled to it and ends when the passed ball touches or is touched by an in-bounds player other than the thrower-in.

Try for Field Goal

SECTION 29. a. A try for field goal is an attempt by a player to score two points by throwing the ball into his basket. The try starts when the player begins the motion which habitually precedes the release of the ball. The try ends when the throw is successful, or it is certain the throw is unsuccessful, or when the thrown ball touches the floor or any player, or when the ball becomes dead.

b. The act of shooting begins simultaneously with the start of the try and ends when the ball is clearly in flight.

Violation

SECTION 30. A violation is a rule infraction of the type listed in Rule 9.

RULE 6—LIVE BALL AND DEAD BALL

Game—How Started

SECTION 1. The game shall be started by a jump ball in the center circle. After any subsequent dead ball, play shall be resumed by a jump ball or by a throw-in or by placing it at the disposal of a free thrower. The ball becomes alive when:

    a. On a jump ball, the ball leaves the official's hand.

    b. On a throw-in, the ball touches or is touched by a player who is in bounds.

    c. On a free throw, the ball is placed at the disposal of the free thrower.

Center Jump

SECTION 2. The ball shall be put in play in the center

circle by a jump between any two opponents:

    a. At the beginning of each half and extra period.

    b. After a double foul.

QUESTION—Does a half or extra period start with a jump ball if a foul occurs before the ball becomes alive? **ANSWER**—No. Any rules statement is made on the assumption that no infraction is involved unless mentioned or implied. If such infraction occurs, the rule governing it is followed in accordance with Rule 4-24.

Other Jumps

SECTION 3. The ball shall be put in play by a jump ball at the center of the restraining circle which is nearest the spot where:

    a. A held ball occurs.

    b. The ball goes out of bounds as in 7-3.

    c. A double free throw violation occurs.

    d. A live ball lodges on a basket support.

    e. The ball becomes dead when neither team is in control and no goal or infraction or end of a period is involved.

In (a) and (b), the jump shall be between the two involved players unless injury or disqualification requires substitution for a jumper, in which case his substitute shall jump. In (c), (d) and (e), the jump shall be between any two opponents.

Position for Jump Ball

SECTION 4. a. For any jump ball, each jumper shall have one or both feet on or inside that half of the jumping circle (imaginary if in a free throw restraining circle) which is farther from his own basket and both feet within the restraining circle.

An official shall then toss the ball upward between the jumpers in a plane at right angles to the side lines, to a height greater than either of them can jump and so that it will drop between them. The ball must be tapped by one or both of the jumpers after it reaches its highest point. If it touches the floor without being tapped by at least one of the jumpers, the official shall toss the ball again.

    b. Neither jumper shall: tap the tossed ball before it reaches its highest point; nor leave the jumping circle until the ball has been tapped; nor catch the jump ball; nor touch it more than twice. The jump ball and these restrictions end when the tapped ball touches one of the eight non-jumpers, the floor, the basket or the backboard.

    c. When the official is ready to make the toss, a nonjumper shall not move onto the circle or change position around the circle, until the ball has left the official's hand.

    d. None of the eight nonjumpers shall have either foot break the plane of the restraining circle cylinder until the ball has been tapped. Teammates may not occupy adjacent positions around the restraining circle if an opponent indicates his desire for one of these positions before the official is ready to toss the ball; nor may any player take a position in any occupied space.

QUESTION—During jump ball, is a jumper required to: (a) face his own basket; and (b) jump and attempt to tap the tossed ball? **ANSWER**—(a) No specific facing is required. However, a jumper must be in the proper half of the jumping circle. (b) No. But if neither jumper taps the ball, it should be tossed again with both jumpers being ordered to jump.

SECTION 5. The ball shall be put in play by a throw-in under circumstances as outlined in Rules 7, 8-5, 9-1 to 11.

SECTION 6. The ball shall be put in play by placing it at the disposal of a free thrower before each free throw.

Dead Ball

SECTION 7. The ball becomes dead or remains dead when:

    a. Any goal is made as in 5-1.

    b. It is apparent the free throw will not be successful: on a free throw for a technical foul or a false double foul, or a free throw which is to be followed by another throw.

    c. Held ball occurs or ball lodges on the basket support.

    d. Official's whistle is blown.

    e. Time expires for a half or extra period.

    f. A foul occurs.

    g. Any floor violation (9-2 to 10) occurs, or there is basket interference (9-11), or there is a free throw violation by the thrower's team (9-1).

Exception 1: The ball does not become dead until the try or tap ends when: (a) d, e, or f occurs while a try for a field goal or a tapped ball by a player toward his basket is in flight; (b) d or f occurs while a try for a free throw is in flight; (c) a foul is committed by an opponent of a player who has started a try for goal (is in the act of shooting) before the foul occurred, provided time did not expire before the ball was in flight (The trying motion must be continuous and begins after the ball comes to rest in the player's hand or hands and is completed when the ball is clearly in flight. The trying motion may include arm, foot, or body movements used by the player when throwing the ball at his basket.), or (d) when the ball is in flight on a try or tap for field goal or during a free throw and a defensive player excessively swings his arms or elbows without contacting an opponent, the ball remains alive.

QUESTION—If the ball is in flight during A's try for field goal or A's tap in flight toward his own basket when time for the period expires, and if the ball is subsequently touched, does goal count if made? **ANSWER**—No. Ball becomes dead when touched while in flight during the try or tap. If it is basket interference (9-11) by B, two points are awarded to A.

Exception 2: The ball does not become dead while it is in the air on a tap by a player toward his basket if: (a) time expires, or (b) a foul is committed, or (c) any opponent of the player making the tap at his basket swings his arms excessively without making contact.

RULE 8—FREE THROW

Positions During Attempt

SECTION 1. When a free throw is awarded, an official shall take the ball to the free throw line of the offended team. After allowing reasonable time for players to take their positions, he shall put the ball in play by placing it at the disposal of the free thrower. The same procedure shall be followed for each free throw of a multiple throw. During a free throw for a personal foul, each of the lane spaces adjacent to the end line shall be occupied by one opponent of the free thrower. A teammate of the free thrower is entitled to the next adjacent lane space on each side and to each other alternate position along each lane line. Not more than one player may occupy any part of a designated lane space. If the ball is to become dead when the last free throw for a specific penalty is not successful, players shall not take positions along the free throw lane.

NOTE—*To avoid disconcerting the free thrower, neither official should stand in the free throw lane or the lane extended.*

Who Attempts

SECTION 2. The free throw or throws awarded because of a personal foul shall be attempted by the offended player. If such player must withdraw because of an injury or disqualification, his substitute shall attempt the throw or throws unless no substitute is available, in which event any teammate may attempt the throw or throws.

NOTE—*See Question [1] under Rule 2-11.*

SECTION 3. The free throw awarded because of a technical foul may be attempted by any player, including an entering substitute, of the offended team.

10-Second Limit

SECTION 4. The try for goal shall be made within 10 seconds after the ball has been placed at the disposal of the free thrower at the free throw line. This shall apply to each free throw.

Next Play

SECTION 5. After a free throw which is not followed by another free throw, the ball shall be put in play by a throw-in: (a) as after a field goal (7-5) if the try is for a personal foul and is successful; or (b) by any player of the free thrower's team from out of bounds at the division line if the free throw is for a technical foul.

Ball in Play if Goal is Missed

SECTION 6. If a free throw for a personal foul is unsuccessful, or if there is a multiple throw for a personal foul (or fouls) and the last free throw is unsuccessful, the ball remains alive.

If there is a multiple throw and both a personal and technical foul are involved, the tries shall be attempted in the order in which the related fouls were called; and if the last try is for a technical foul, the ball shall be put in play as after any technical foul.

Ball in Play after False Double Foul

SECTION 7. After the last free throw following a false double foul (4-11-c), the ball shall be put in play as if the penalty for the last foul of the false double foul were the only one administered.

QUESTION—Two free throws are awarded to A1; and before time is in, two free throws are awarded to Team B for a technical foul on the coach of Team A. What is the correct procedure? **ANSWER**—With no players lined up, A1 shall attempt his two free throws; and Team B shall attempt its two free throws, after which the ball is awarded to Team B out of bounds at the division line.

RULE 9—VIOLATIONS AND PENALTIES

Free Throw

SECTION 1. A player shall not violate the following free throw provisions:

a. The try shall be attempted from within the free

throw circle and behind the free throw line.

b. After the ball is placed at the disposal of a free thrower:

l. He shall throw within 10 seconds and in such a way that the ball enters the basket or touches the ring before the free throw ends.

2. No opponent shall disconcert the free thrower.

3. No player shall enter or leave a lane space.

4. The free thrower shall not have either foot beyond the vertical plane of that edge of the free throw line which is farther from the basket; nor any lines which bound the semicircle; and no other player of either team shall have either foot beyond the vertical plane or cylinder of the outside edge of any lane boundary, nor beyond the vertical plane of any edge of the space (two inches [5.08cm] by 36 inches [91.44cm] designated by a lane space mark or the space (12 inches [30.48cm] by 36 inches [91.44cm]) designated by a neutral zone mark. The restrictions in (3) and (4) apply until the ball touches the ring or backboard or until the free throw ends.

c. An opponent of the free thrower shall occupy each lane space adjacent to the end line during the try, and no teammate of the free thrower may occupy either of these lane spaces.

PENALTY—[1] If violation is by the free thrower or his teammate only, no point can be scored by that throw. Ball becomes dead when violation occurs. Ball is awarded out of bounds on the sideline to the free thrower's team opposite center circle after a technical foul, and to any opponent out of bounds at either end of the free throw line extended after a personal foul.

[2] If violation is by the free thrower's opponent only: if the try is successful, the goal counts and violation is disregarded; if it is not successful, and the ball becomes dead when the free throw ends, a substitute throw shall be attempted by the same thrower under conditions the same as for the throw for which it is substituted.

[3] If there is a violation by *each* team, ball becomes dead when violation by the free thrower's team occurs, no point can be scored, and play shall be resumed by a jump between any two opponents in the nearest circle.

The out-of-bounds provision in penalty item [1] and the jump-ball provision in penalty item [3] do not apply if the free throw is to be followed by another free throw, or if there are free throws by both teams. In penalty item [3], if an opponent of the thrower touches the free throw before it has touched the ring, the violation for failure to touch the ring is ignored or if a violation by the free thrower follows disconcertion, a substitute free throw shall be awarded.

QUESTION—During a free throw by A1, B1 pushes A2 and also B1 or B2 is in the lane too soon. ANSWER—If the free throw is successful, penalize the foul. I the free throw is not successful, award a substitute free throw and also penalize the foul.

SECTION 2. A player shall not cause the ball to go out of bounds.

QUESTION—Dribbler in control steps on or outside a boundary, but does not touch the ball while he is out of bounds. Is this a violation? ANSWER—Yes.

Throw-in
SECTION 3. A player shall not violate provisions governing the throw-in. The thrower-in shall not:

a. Leave the designated throw-in spot.

b. Fail to pass the ball directly into the court so that after it crosses the boundary line it touches or is touched by another player on the court before going out of bounds.

c. Consume more than five seconds from the time the throw-in starts until it touches or is touched by a player on the court.

d. Carry the ball onto the court;

e. Touch it in the court before it has touched another player.

f. Throw the ball so that it enters the basket before touching anyone.

No player shall:

g. Have any part of his person beyond the vertical inside plane of any end line or side line before the ball has crossed the line.

h. Become the thrower-in or be out of bounds after an official has designated another player.

QUESTION—During a throw-in, A1 steps or reaches through the boundary plane while holding the ball. ANSWER—Violation. Allowance should be made if space is limited.

Kicking the Ball
SECTION 4. A player shall not run with the ball, kick it, strike it with the fist or cause it to enter and pass through the basket from below.

NOTE—*Kicking the ball is a violation only when it is a positive act; accidentally striking the ball with the foot or leg is not a violation.*

QUESTION—What is kicking the ball? ANSWER—Kicking the ball is striking it intentionally with the knee or any part of the leg or foot below the knee. It is a fundamental of basketball that the ball must be played with the hands.

Double Dribble

SECTION 5. A player shall not dribble a second time after his first dribble has ended, unless it is after he has lost control because of: (a) a try for field goal; or (b) a bat by an opponent; or (c) a pass or fumble which has then touched or been touched by another player.

Jump Ball

SECTION 6. A player shall not violate any provision of 6-4. If both teams simultaneously commit violations during the jump ball, or if the official makes a bad toss, the toss should be repeated.

Three-Second Rule

SECTION 7. A player shall not remain for more than three seconds in that part of his free throw lane between the end boundary and the farther edge of the free throw line while the ball is in control of his team in his frontcourt. Allowance shall be made for a player who, having been in the restricted area for less than three seconds, dribbles in to try for goal.

QUESTION—Does the three-second restriction apply: (a) to a player who has only one foot touching the lane boundary; or (b) while the ball is dead or is in flight during a try? ANSWER—(a) Yes, the line is part of the lane. (b) No, the team is not in control.

Ten-Second Rule

SECTION 8. A player shall not be (and his team shall not be) in continuous control of a ball which is in his backcourt for more than 10 consecutive seconds.

Ball in Backcourt

SECTION 9. A player shall not be the first to touch a ball which he or a teammate caused to go from frontcourt to backcourt by being the last to touch the ball while it was in control of his team and before it went to the backcourt.

Exception: It is not a violation when after a jump ball at the center circle, a player is the first to secure control of the ball while both feet are off the floor, and he then returns to the floor with one or both feet in the backcourt.

QUESTION—A receives pass in his frontcourt and throws ball to his backcourt where ball: (a) is touched by a teammate; or (b) goes directly out of bounds; or (c) lies or bounces with all players hesitating to touch it. ANSWER—Violation when touched in (a). In (b) it is a violation for going out of bounds. In (c) ball is alive so that B may secure control. If A touches ball first, it is a violation. The ball continues to be in team control of A, and if A does not touch it the 10-second count starts when the ball arrives in the backcourt.

SECTION 10. A player shall not excessively swing his arms or elbows, even though there is no contact with an opponent. (See Comments.)

PENALTY—(Sections 2 to 10)—Ball becomes dead or remains dead when violation occurs. Ball is awarded to a nearby opponent for a throw-in at the out-of-bounds spot nearest the violation. If the ball passes through a basket during the dead ball period immediately following a violation, no point can be scored and the ball is awarded to an opponent out of bounds at either end of that free throw line extended nearer the goal through which the ball was thrown.

Basket Interference and Goal Tending

SECTION 11. a. A player shall not touch the ball or basket when the ball is on or within either basket.
b. A player shall not touch the ball when it is touching the cylinder having the ring as its lower base.
c. A player shall not touch the ball during a field goal try while it is in its downward flight entirely above the basket ring level and has the possibility of entering the basket in flight.
d. A player shall not touch a ball which has been tapped by a player toward his basket while the ball is in its downward flight entirely above the basket ring level and has the possibility of entering the basket in flight.

If the ball has touched or been touched by a player before it began its downward flight or if the ball has touched the ring, the restrictions in (c) and (d) do not apply.

Exception: In (a) or (b), if a player has his hand legally in contact with the ball, it is not a violation if his contact with the ball continues after it enters a basket cylinder, or if, in such action, he touches the basket.

PENALTY—If violation is at the opponent's basket, offended team is awarded one point if during a free throw and two points in any other case. The crediting of the score and subsequent procedure is the same as if the awarded score had resulted from the ball having gone through the basket, except that the official shall hand the ball to a player of the team entitled to the throw-in.

If the violation is at a team's own basket, no points can be scored and the ball is awarded to the offended team at the out-of-bounds spot on the side at either end of the free throw line extended.

If the violation results from touching the ball while it is in the basket after entering from below, the ball is

awarded out of bounds to the opponent and no points are scored.

If there is a violation by both teams, play shall be resumed by a jump ball between any two opponents in the nearest circle.

QUESTION—While the ball is in flight during a try for field goal by A or is in flight toward the basket of Team A following a tap by A, a teammate of A pushes an opponent. After this personal foul, the ball is on the ring when B bats it away. Which infraction should be penalized? ANSWER —In each situation award two points to A. Then penalize for personal foul.